EASY GUITAR TAB EDITION

EASY GUITAR ANTHOLOGY

GREEN DAY

20 GREATEST HITS

ALBUM ARTWORK:

American Idiot © 2004 Reprise Records for the U.S. and
WEA International Inc. for the world outside the U.S.

Shenanigans © 2002 Reprise Records for the U.S. and
WEA International Inc. for the world outside the U.S.

Warning © 2000 Reprise Records for the U.S. and
WEA International Inc. for the world outside the U.S.

Nimrod © 1997 Reprise Records for the U.S. and
WEA International Inc. for the world outside the U.S.

Insomniac © 1995 Reprise Records for the U.S. and
WEA International Inc. for the world outside the U.S.

Dookie © 1994 Reprise Records for the U.S. and
WEA International Inc. for the world outside the U.S.

Kerplunk © 1991 Lookout Records

EXCLUSIVELY DISTRIBUTED BY

ISBN: 978-0-7390-4069-0

CONTENTS

AMERICAN IDIOT

Words by BILLIE JOE
Music by GREEN DAY

4

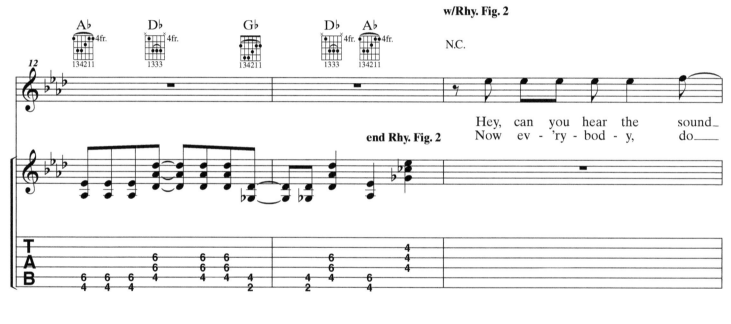

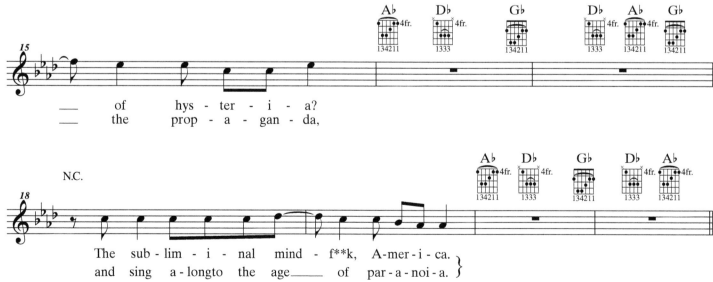

%: *Chorus:*

Wel-come to a new___ kind of ten - sion all a-cross the a-

- li - en - a - tion___ where ev-'ry-thing is - n't meant___ to___ be o -

kay.___ Tel - e - vi - sion dreams___

___ of to - mor - row, we're not the ones___ who're meant to fol - low,___

To Coda

N.C.

___ for that's e - nough___ to ar - gue.

1.
w/Rhy. Fig. 1

2.
w/Rhy. Fig. 1, *2 times*

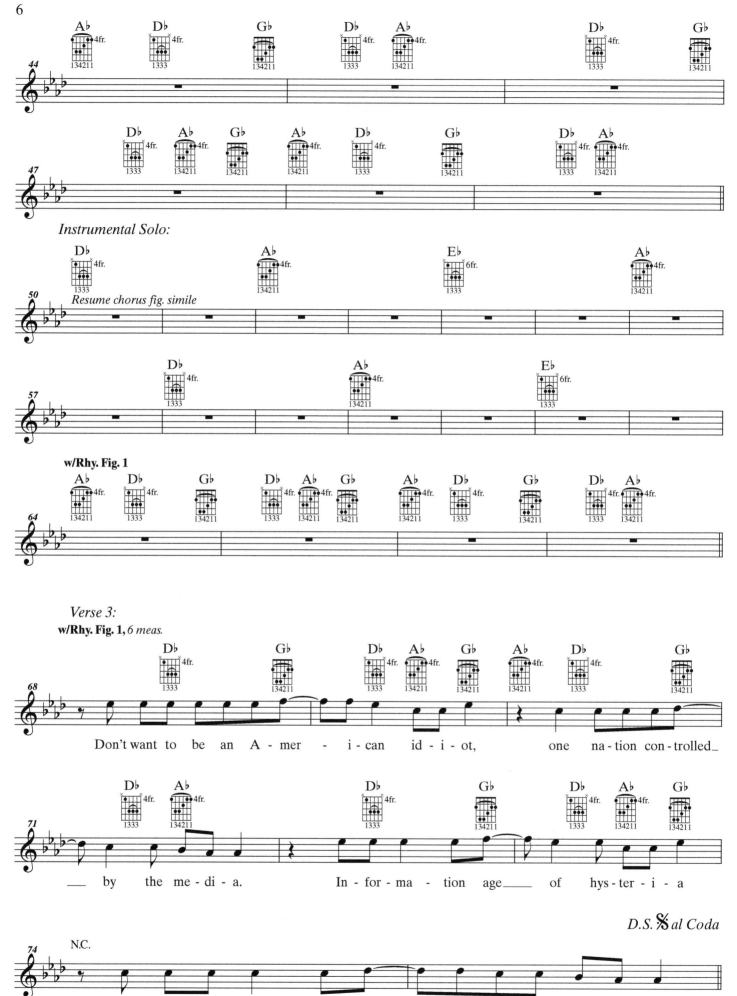

Instrumental Solo:

Resume chorus fig. simile

w/Rhy. Fig. 1

Verse 3:

w/Rhy. Fig. 1, *6 meas.*

Don't want to be an A - mer - i - can id - i - ot, one na - tion con - trolled___

___ by the me - di - a. In - for - ma - tion age___ of hys - ter - i - a

D.S. %al Coda

N.C.

is call - ing out to id - i - ot A - mer - i - ca.

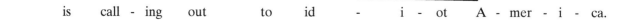

Outro:

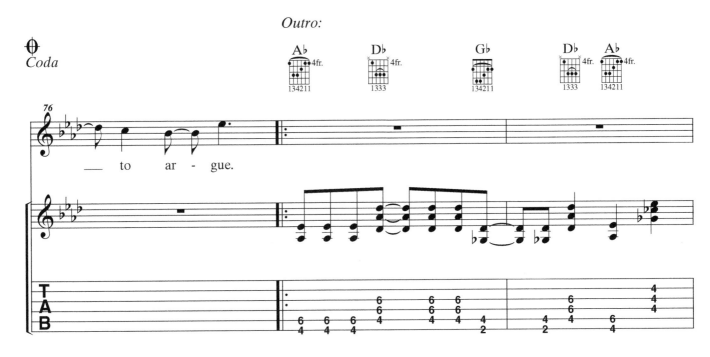

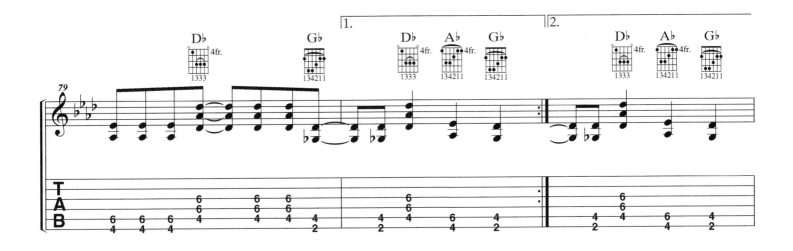

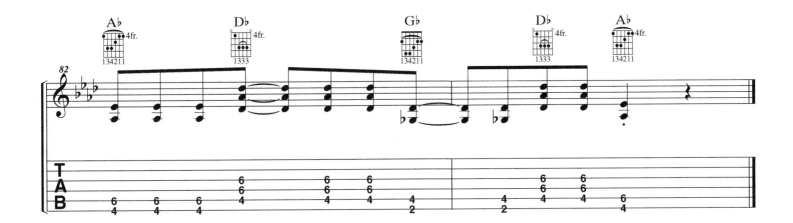

BOULEVARD OF BROKEN DREAMS

Words by BILLIE JOE
Music by GREEN DAY

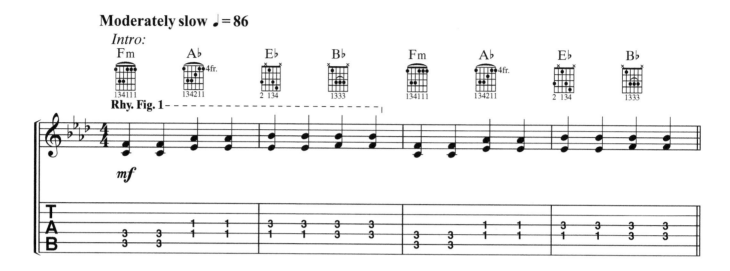

BRAIN STEW

To match recorded key, tune down 1/2 step:

Lyrics by BILLIE JOE
Music by GREEN DAY

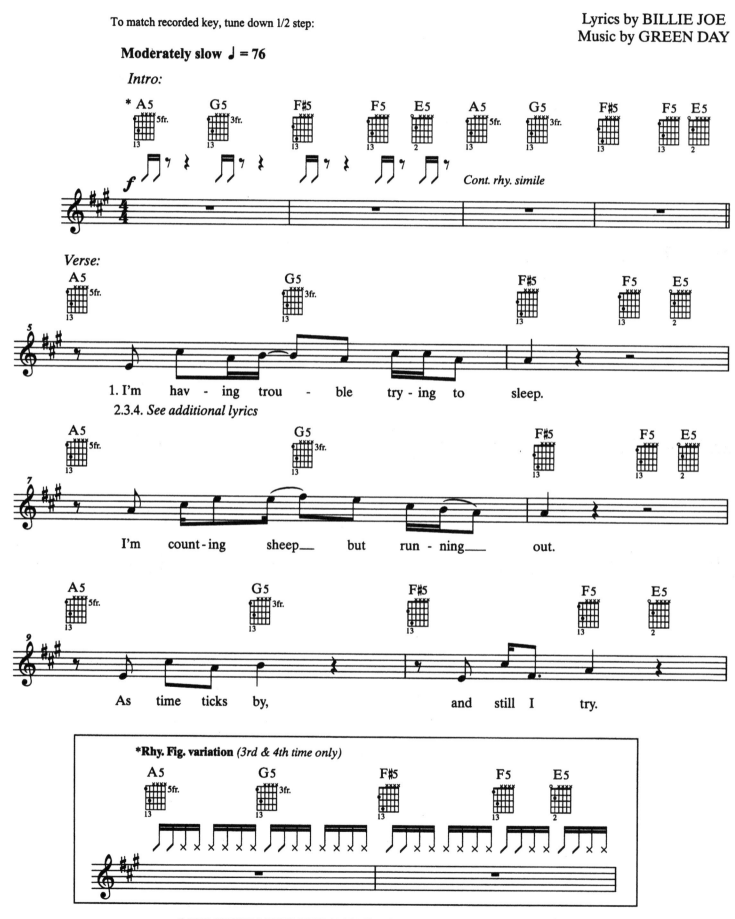

Verse 2:
My eyes feel like they're gonna bleed,
Dried up and bulging out my skull.
My mouth is dry,
My face is numb.
F***ed up and spun out in my room.
On my own.
Here we go.
(To Verse 3:)

Verse 3:
My mind is set on overdrive.
The clock is laughing in my face.
A crooked spine,
My sense is dulled.
Passed the point of delirium.
On my own.
Here we go.
(To Verse 4:)

Verse 4:
My eyes feel like they're gonna bleed,
Dried up and bulging out my skull.
My mouth is dry,
My face is numb.
F***ed up and spun out in my room.
On my own.
Here we go.
(To Outro:)

BASKET CASE

Lyrics by BILLIE JOE
Music by GREEN DAY

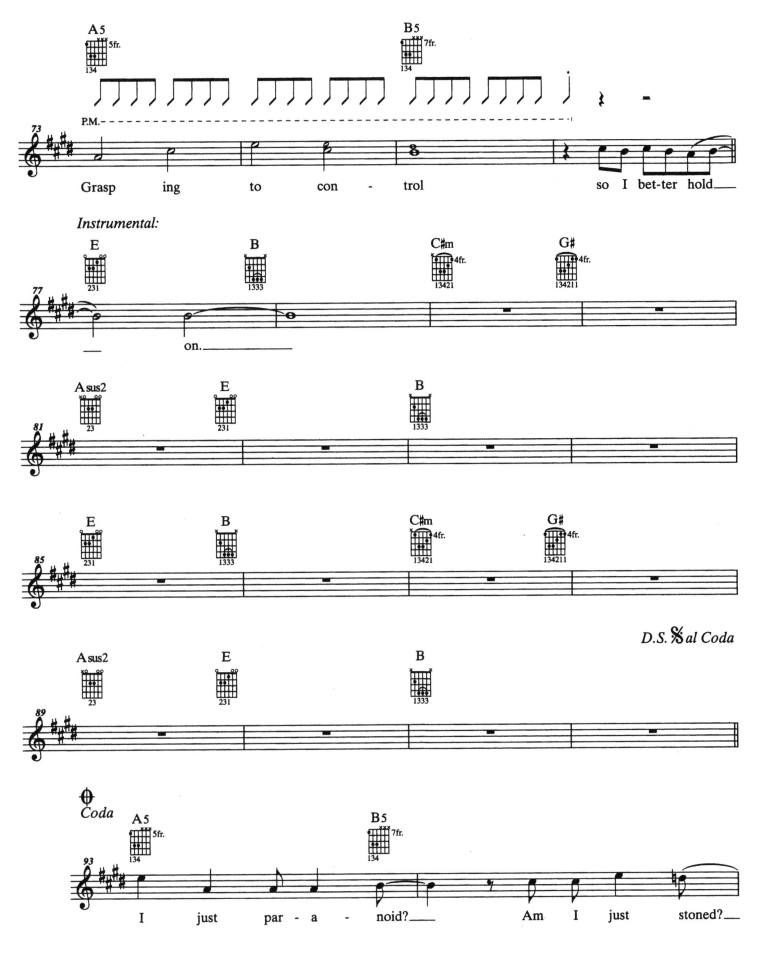

Play 3 times

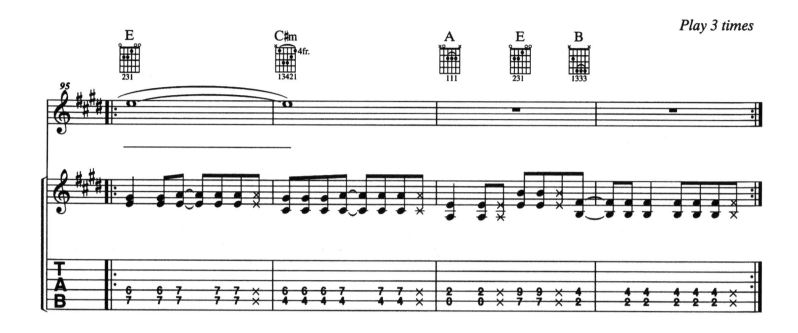

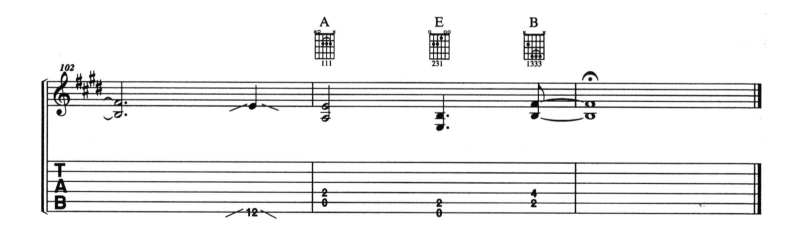

ESPIONAGE

Music by GREEN DAY

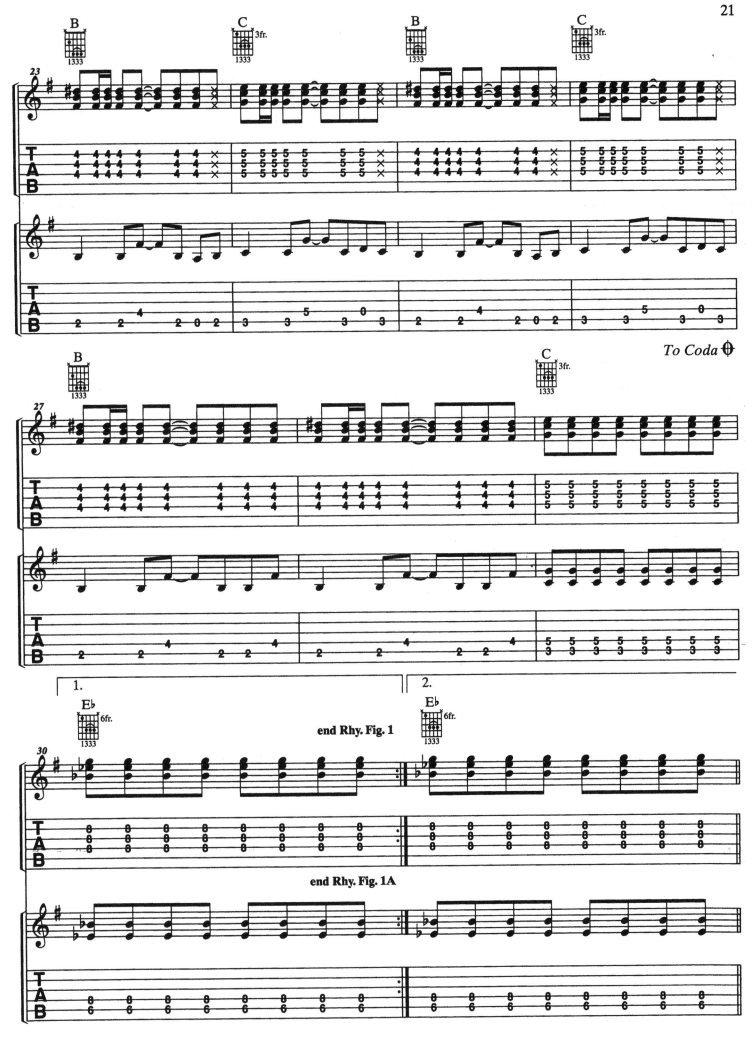

To Coda ✛

end Rhy. Fig. 1

end Rhy. Fig. 1A

B

w/Rhy. Figs. 1 *(Elec. Gtr. 1)* **& 1A** *(Elec. Gtr. 2)*

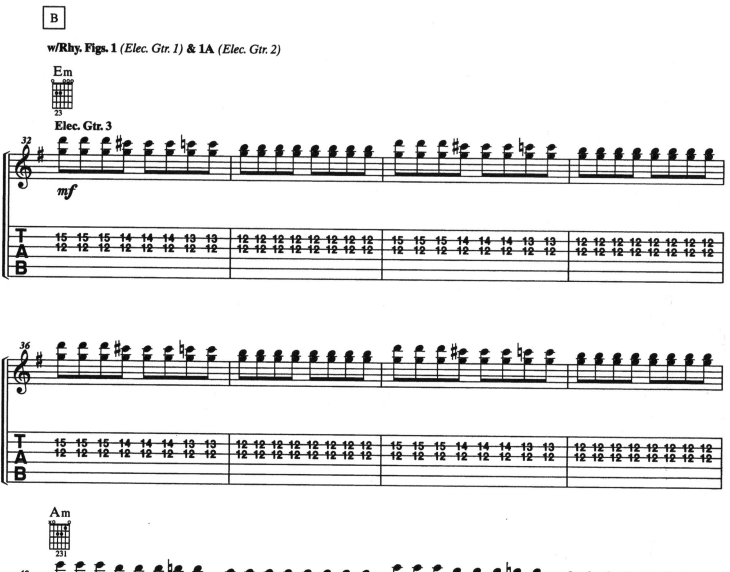

Elec. Gtr. 3

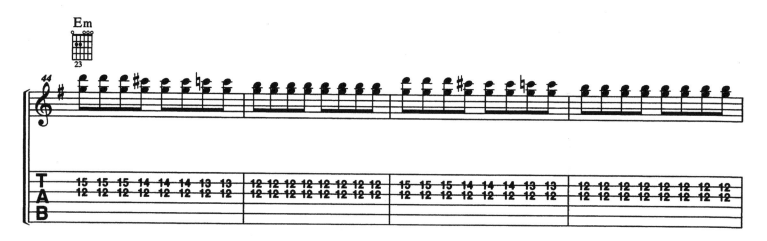

Midtro:

D.S. % al Coda

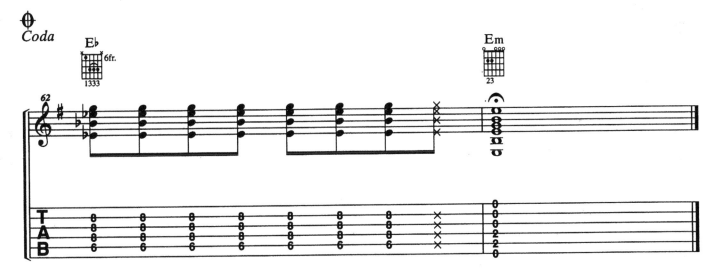

Coda

GOOD RIDDANCE (TIME OF YOUR LIFE)

Lyrics by BILLIE JOE
Music by BILLIE JOE and GREEN DAY

HITCHIN' A RIDE

Lyrics by BILLIE JOE
Music by GREEN DAY

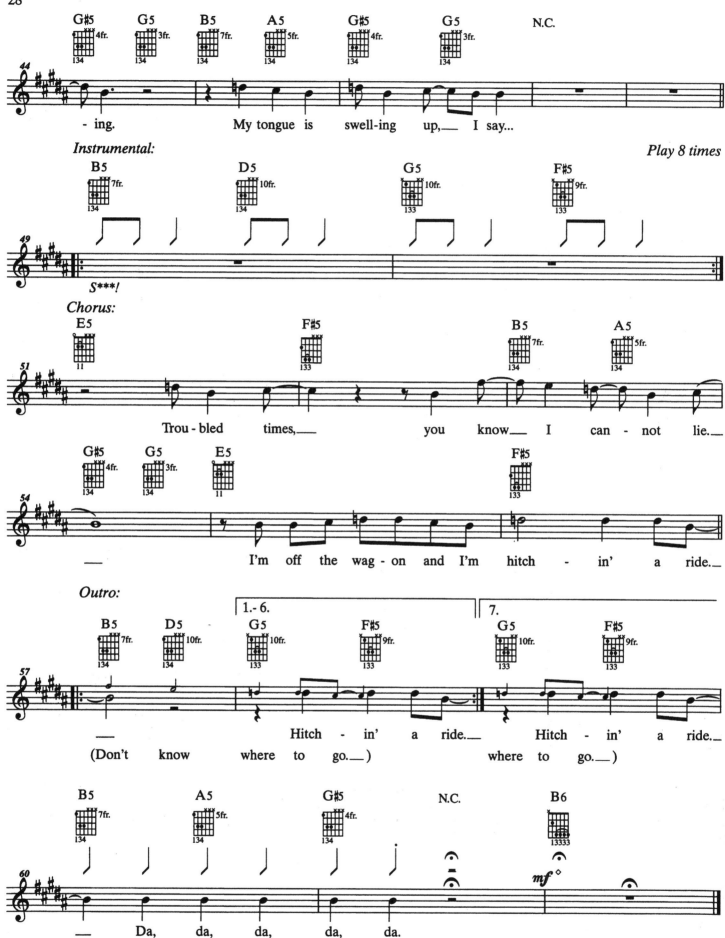

HOLIDAY

Words by BILLIE JOE
Music by GREEN DAY

*To match recorded key, place capo at 1st fret.

Guitar Solo:

Bridge:

The rep - re - sen - ta - tive from Cal - i - for - nia has the floor.

Zieg Heil to the Pres - i - dent gas - man, bombs a - way is your pun - ish - ment.

Pul - ver - ize the Eif - fel Tow - ers, who crit - i - cize your gov - ern - ment.

Bang, bang goes the bro - ken glass and kill all the fags that don't a - gree.

Tri - als by fire___ set - ting fire___ is not a way that's

meant for me. Just 'cause...
(Hey, hey, hey, hey,

just 'cause, be - cause we're out - laws, yeah.
hey, hey, hey, hey.)

Holiday - 5 - 5
25507

JADED

Lyrics by BILLIE JOE
Music by GREEN DAY

LONGVIEW

rics by BILLIE JOE
usic by GREEN DAY

MACY'S DAY PARADE

Words by BILLIE JOE
Music by GREEN DAY

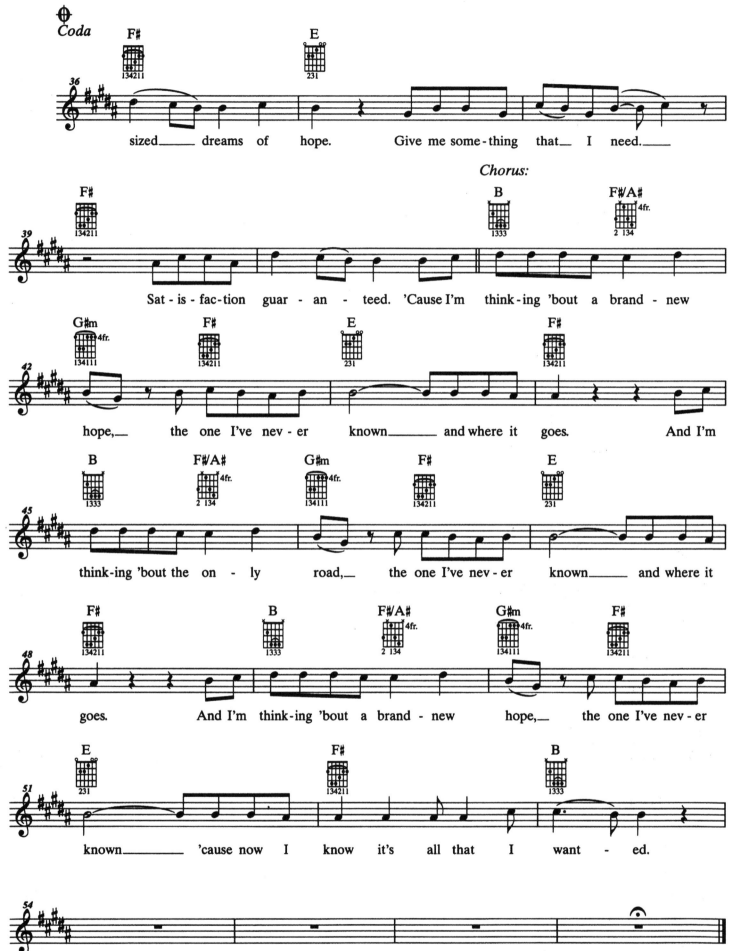

Coda

sized____ dreams of hope. Give me some-thing that__ I need.__

Chorus:

Sat-is-fac-tion guar-an-teed. 'Cause I'm think-ing 'bout a brand-new

hope,__ the one I've nev-er known_____ and where it goes. And I'm

think-ing 'bout the on-ly road,__ the one I've nev-er known_____ and where it

goes. And I'm think-ing 'bout a brand-new hope,__ the one I've nev-er

known_____ 'cause now I know it's all that I want-ed.

MINORITY

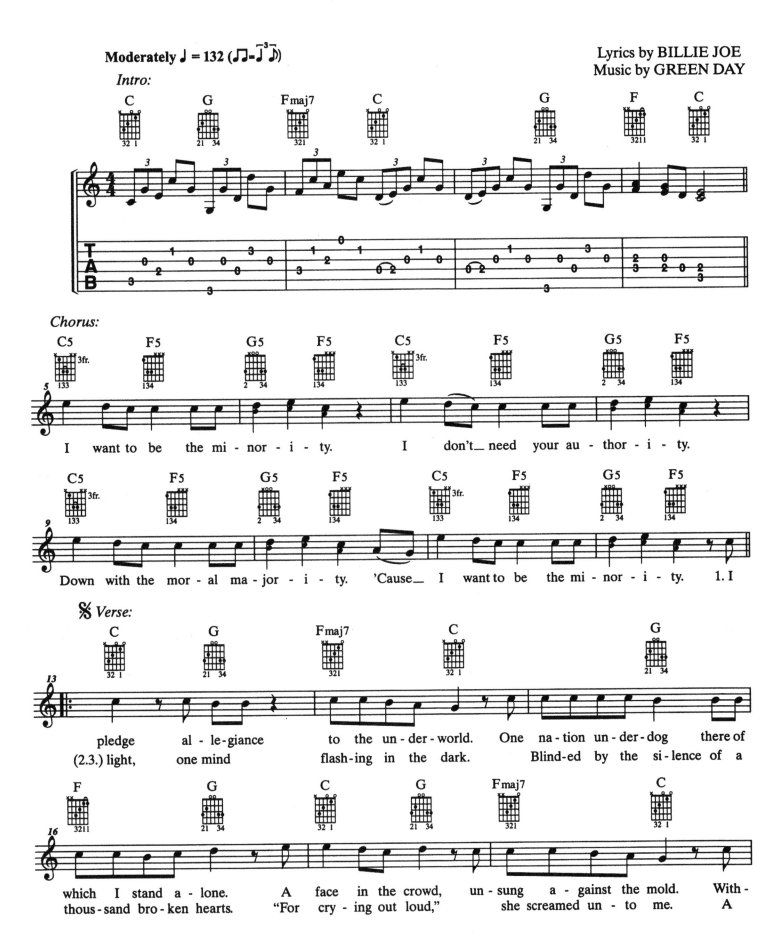

NICE GUYS FINISH LAST

Lyrics by BILLIE JOE
Music by BILLIE JOE and GREEN DAY

Moderately fast ♩ = 188

Intro:

Verse:

1. Nice guys fin-ish last.___ You're
2. Liv-ing on com-mand.___ You're

run-ning out of gas.___ Your sym-pa-thy will get___ you left___ be-
shak-ing lots of hands.___ You're kiss-ing up and bleed-ing all___ your___

48

Interlude:

Chorus:

Oh,— nice guys fin-ish last,— when you are the out-cast.— Don't pat— your-self on the back— — you might break your spine.— Oh,—

STUCK WITH ME

To match recorded key, tune down 1/2 step:

Fast ♩ = 194

Lyrics by BILLIE JOE
Music by GREEN DAY

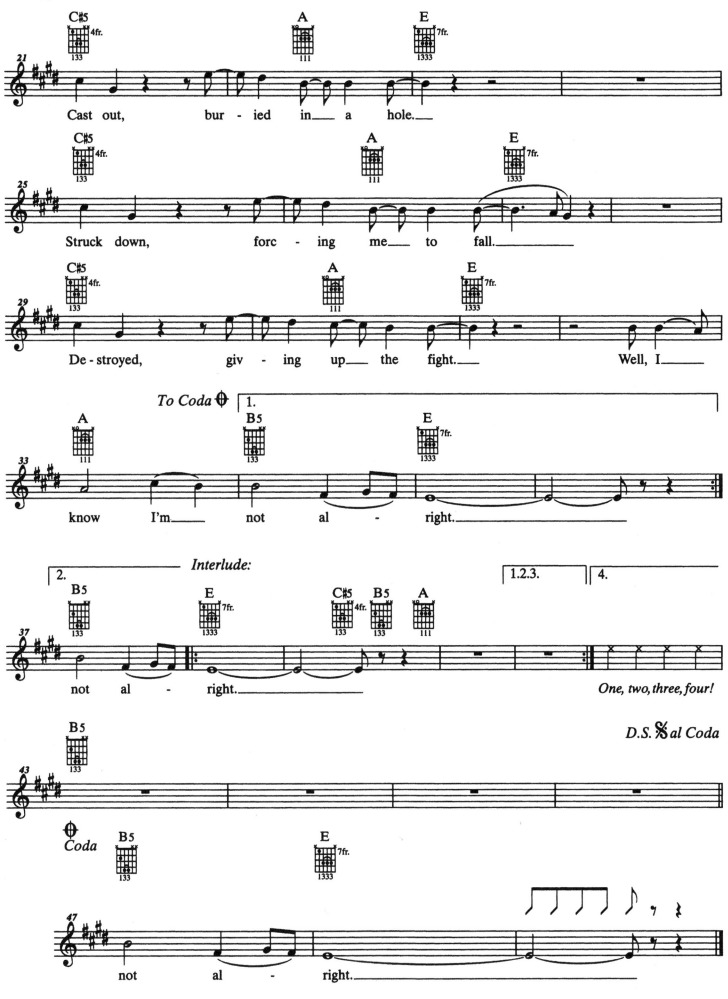

WAITING

To match recorded key, tune down 1/2 step:

Words and Music by BILLIE JOE,
ANTHONY HATCH and GREEN DAY

Moderately ♩ = 134

Intro:

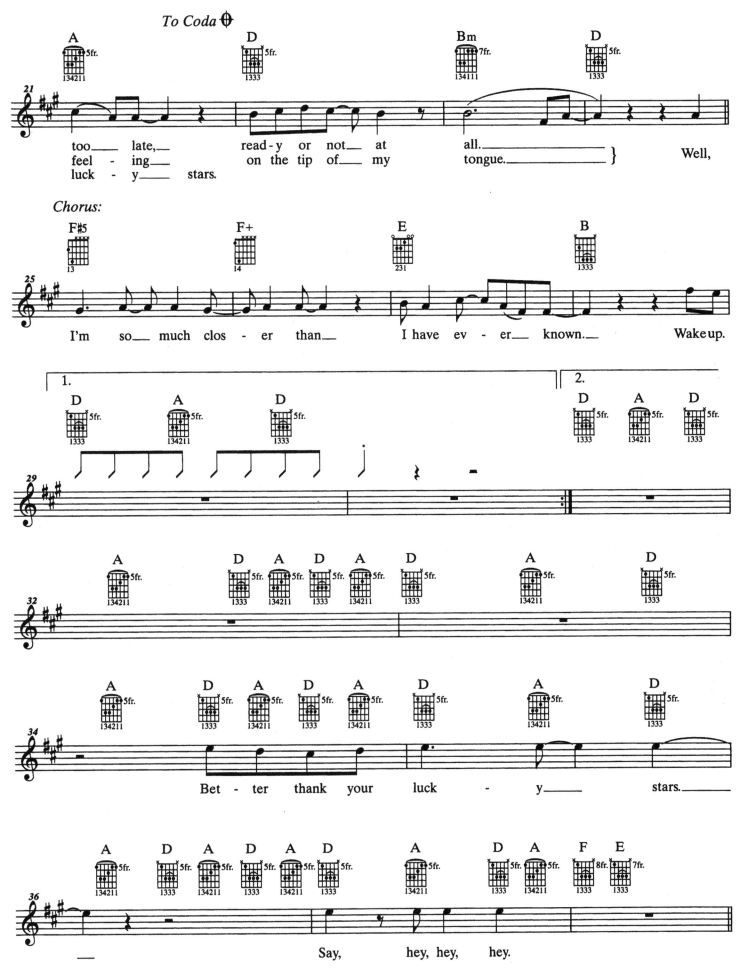

Interlude:

Midtro:

I've___ been___ wait - ing a life - time for___ this___

mo - ment to come.___ I'm des - tined___ for an - y - thing___ at

D.S. 𝄋 *al Coda*

all._____

Coda

WAKE ME UP WHEN SEPTEMBER ENDS

Words by BILLIE JOE
Music by GREEN DAY

Wake Me Up When September Ends - 3 - 1
25507

58

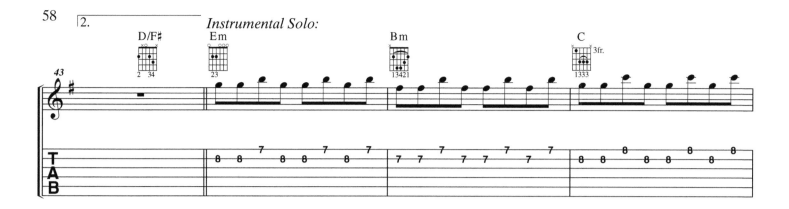

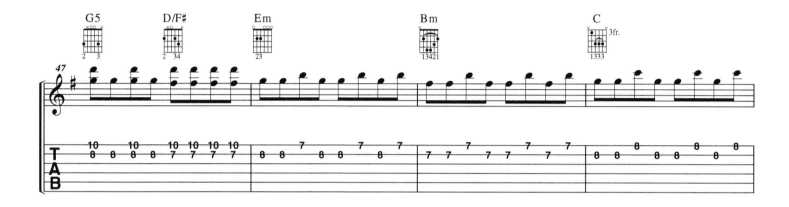

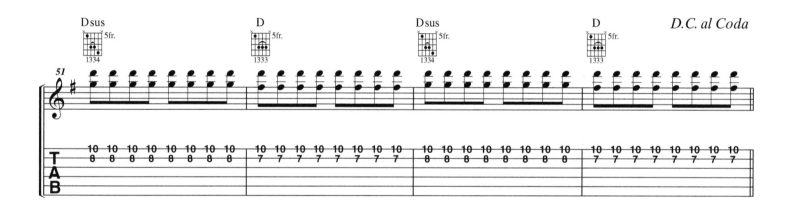

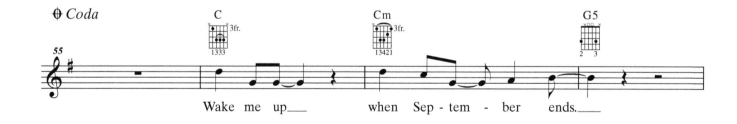

Wake me up___ when Sep - tem - ber ends.___

Wake me up___ when Sep - tem - ber ends.___

Wake Me Up When September Ends - 3 - 3
25507

WALKING CONTRADICTION

Lyrics by BILLIE JOE
Music by GREEN DAY

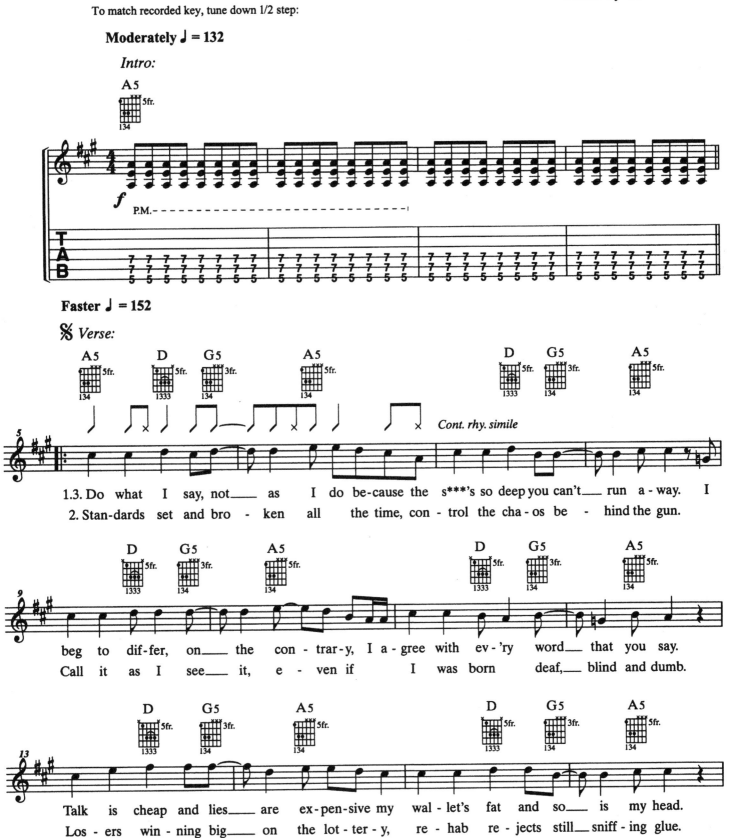

To match recorded key, tune down 1/2 step:

Moderately ♩ = 132

Intro:

Faster ♩ = 152

𝄋 *Verse:*

1.3. Do what I say, not___ as I do be-cause the s***'s so deep you can't___ run a-way. I
2. Stan-dards set and bro - ken all the time, con - trol the cha - os be - hind the gun.

beg to dif-fer, on___ the con - trar-y, I a-gree with ev - 'ry word___ that you say.
Call it as I see___ it, e - ven if I was born deaf,___ blind and dumb.

Talk is cheap and lies___ are ex-pen-sive my wal - let's fat and so___ is my head.
Los - ers win - ning big___ on the lot - ter-y, re - hab re - jects still___ sniff - ing glue.

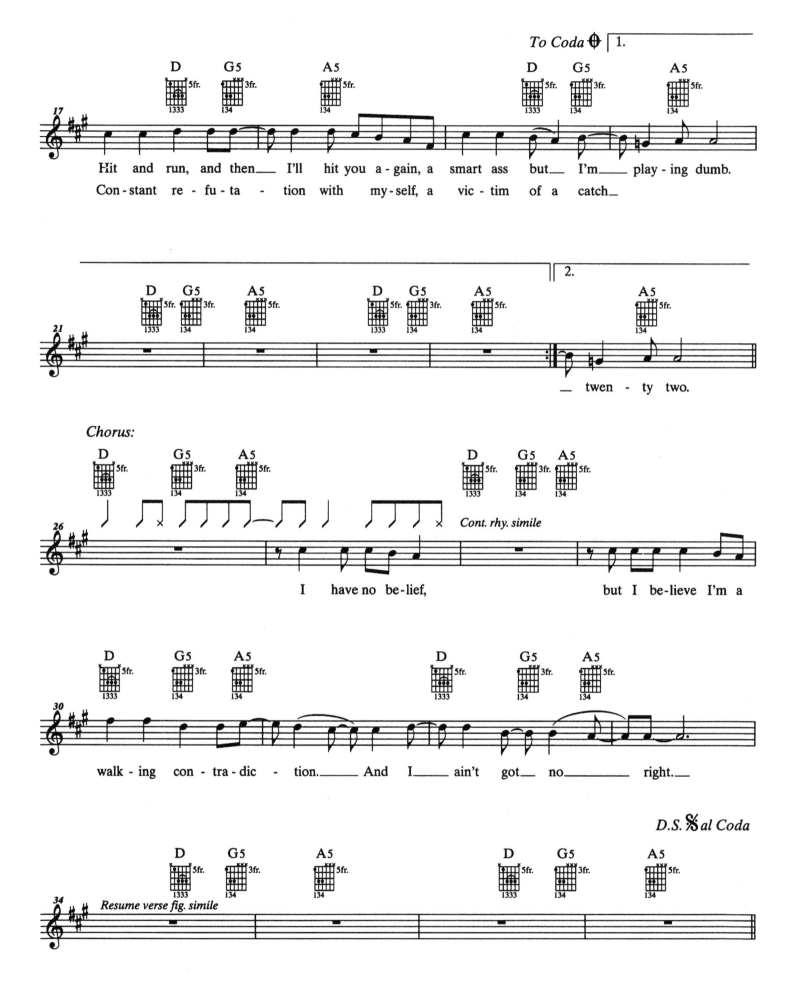

WARNING

Words by BILLIE JOE
Music by GREEN DAY

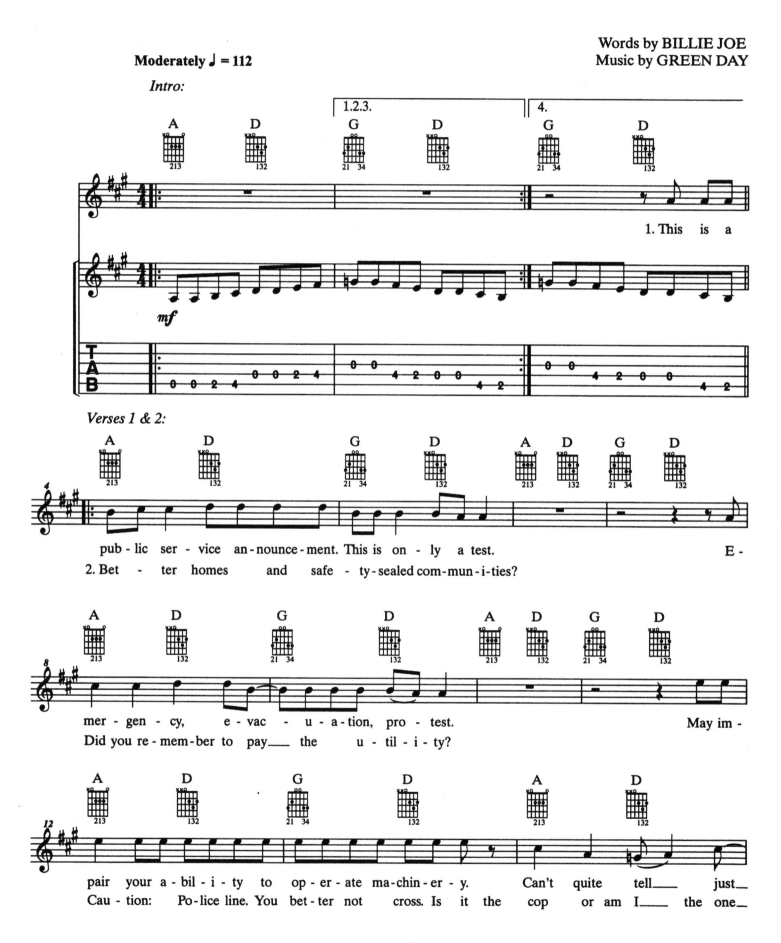

64

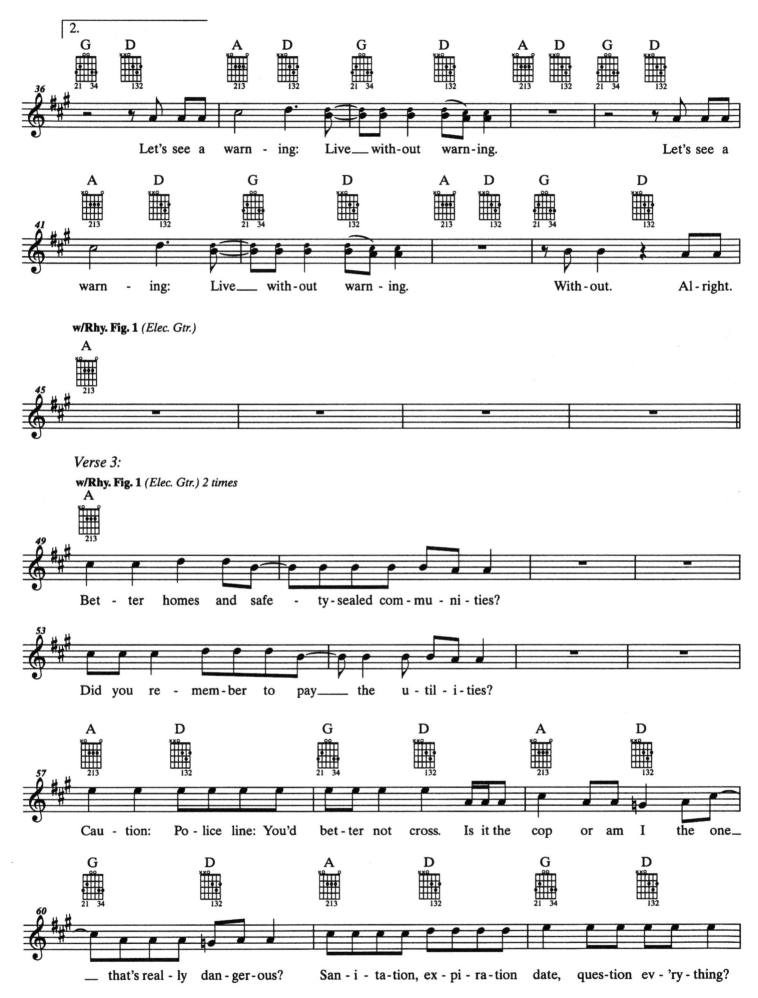

WHEN I COME AROUND

Lyrics by BILLIE JOE
Music by GREEN DAY

To match recorded key, tune down ½ step:

Moderately ♩ = 100

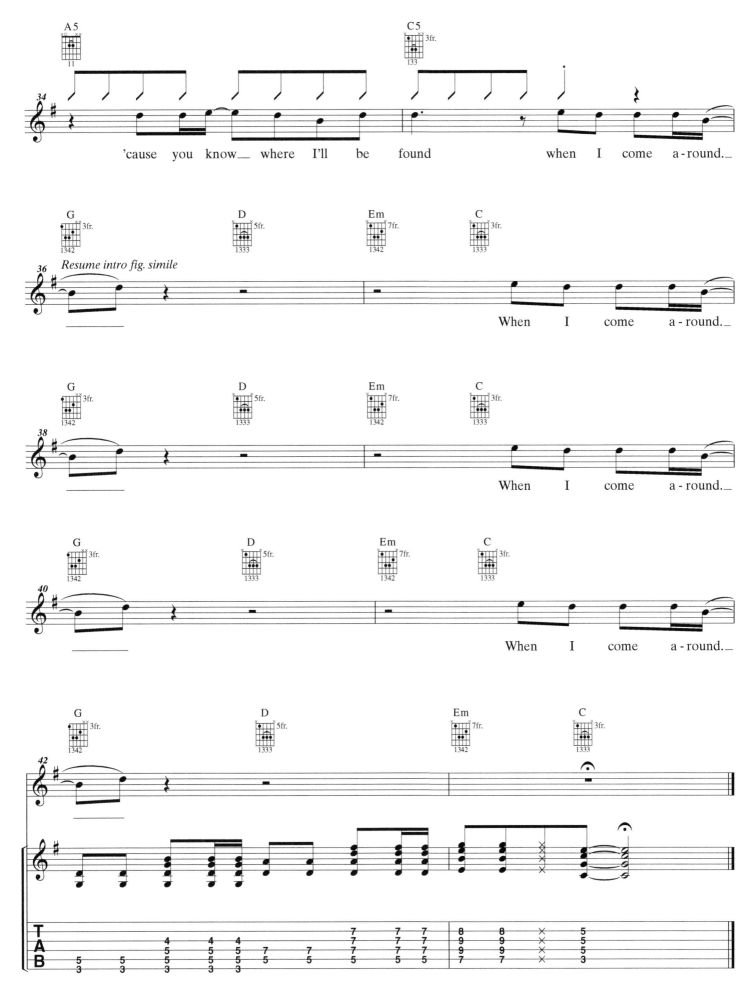

WELCOME TO PARADISE

Lyrics by BILLIE JOE
Music by GREEN DAY

To match recorded key, tune down 1/2 step:

Moderately fast ♩ = 176

Intro: *Play 4 times* 𝄋 *Verse:*

1. Dear moth-er, can___ you hear___ me

2.3. *See additional lyrics*

whin - ing? It's been three whole___ weeks since___ that

I have left your home.___ This sud-den fear___ has left___ me

trem - bling 'cause now it seems___ that I___ am out here on my own___

___ and I'm feel - ing so a - lone._____

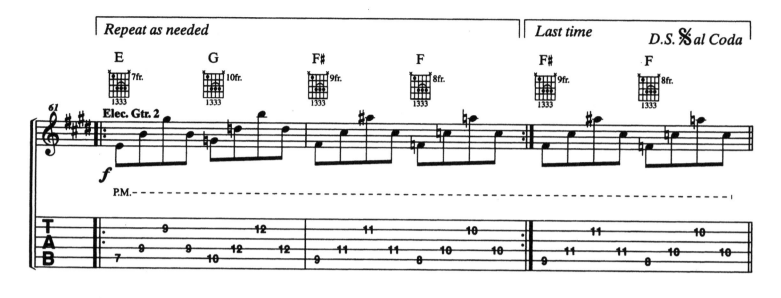

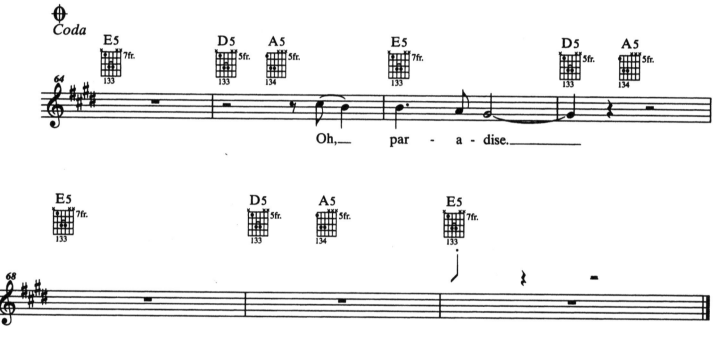

Oh,___ par - a - dise._____

Verse 2:
A gunshot rings out at the station,
Another urchin snaps and left dead on his own.
It makes me wonder why I'm still here.
For some strange reason it's now feeling like my home
And I'm never gonna go.
(To Chorus:)

Verse 3:
Dear mother, can you hear me laughing?
It's been six whole months since I have left your home.
It makes me wonder why I'm still here.
For some strange reason it's now feeling like my home
And I'm never gonna go.
(To Chorus:)